THE SEVEN HUMAN TEMPERAMENTS

THE SEVEN HUMAN TEMPERAMENTS

GEOFFREY HODSON

THE THEOSOPHICAL PUBLISHING HOUSE
Adyar, Madras 600 020, India
Wheaton, Ill., USA ● London, England

© The Theosophical
Publishing House, Adyar, 1952

First Published 1952
First to Sixth Reprint 1953-1981
Seventh Reprint 1987

ISBN   81-7059-052-3 (cloth)
ISBN   81-7059-053-1 (paper)

Printed at the Vasanta Press,
The Theosophical Society
Adyar, Madras 600 020, India

ACKNOWLEDGMENT

I acknowledge with gratitude the great help received in preparing this book from my valued friend, Miss M. G. Fraser, of Auckland, New Zealand.

CONTENTS

CHAPTER I

THE SIGNIFICANCE OF NUMBER

As our knowledge of human nature grows, we cannot fail to be impressed by the great diversity of human gifts, by the richness of individuality amongst mankind, the almost infinite variety of human beings, the complexity of human nature. Humanity includes the dauntless explorer and the gentle nun, the soldier and the hermit, the monk and the recluse, the politician, the businessman and woman outwardly active in world affairs, the scientist and the scholar immersed in their researches. All these and many other diverse and opposite types go to the making up of mankind.

Is there a key by means of which human nature may be understood and this infinite variety and vast potentiality of man be comprehended and reduced to order? Theosophy answers " yes", and further says that the key is numerical, the governing number being seven. Thus there are seven main types of human beings, each with its outstanding natural attributes and qualities. All qualities and powers are within every human being, but in each of the seven main types there is a preponderant tendency. Knowledge of these seven types and their corresponding attributes provides a key to the understanding of human nature.

Since this key is numerical in character, it becomes necessary to advance the Theosophical teaching concerning numerical progression in cosmogenesis.

Numerically, the active Source of all life and all from is represented by the number One, and the passive source, negative existence, the Absolute, by Zero, Nothing. According to occult cosmogony, the next step in the creative process is the emergence from the One of Its inherent positive and negative aspects or masculine and femine potencies. The One becomes Two or androgyne. These Two interact to produce the Third Aspect of the threefold manifested Logos.[1] These Three in turn unite in all their possible combinations to produce seven groups of three. In three of these groups, one of the three predominates; in three others, two predominate and in the seventh, all are equally manifest. Since divine consciousness is focused and active in each of these Emanations, they are regarded as finite Beings or " Persons ". From the Three Persons of the Blessed Trinity, the Seven emerge, who are known in Christian Cosmogony as the Seven Mighty Spirits before the Throne, in Judaism as the Seven Sephiroth and in Theosophy as the Seven Planetary Logoi, each the Logos of a Scheme of seven Chains of globes.[2]

---

[1] *Logos.* The manifested Deity who speaks the creative Word whereby universes spring into being; life is the outward expression of the Causeless Cause which is ever concealed. Adapted from *The Secret Doctrine* and *The Theosophical Glossary*, H. P. Blavatsky.

[2] Vide *First Principles of Theosophy*, C. Jinarajadasa.

The physical arm of man may be used as an analogy for this numerical basis of manifestation. The arm itself is a single member and yet is sevenfold. Primarily it consists of three parts: the upper arm, the forearm and the hand. Though one, the arm is also threefold. The hand, however, has five fingers, making, with forearm and upper arm, seven parts, each, like the Seven Sephiroth, with its appropriate function.

Theosophy thus teaches that all manifested divine Power, Life and Consciousness, and so all human Monads[1] or Spirits, radiate from the One Source and pass through the Three and the Seven. In their passage through the Three and the Seven, these three Emanations of the Logos, divine Power, Life and Consciousness, are impressed with the special quality of that One, of the Three " Persons ", and the Seven Sephiroth through which they pass, are attuned to their vibratory frequency or chord and are stained with their particular colour. The colour of the spectrum and divine attribute which each of these Sephiroths represents is accentuated in each projected Monadic Ray[2] and thereafter predominates over the other six.

The universe itself is sevenfold, and the notes of its chord are seven in number, each note representing both a mode of manifestation of the Supreme and an eternal truth. The seven notes are variously described. The first and the seventh are the Alpha and Omega of

[1] *Monad*. The one indivisible Self—the unity; the eternal, immortal and indestructible human spirit. See Chap. X.

[2] *Ibid.*, Chapter X.

manifested Life; they are the first and the last, the centre and the circumference containing the whole. The first is the primordial Source, the point, the positive power of the universe. In the Logos, it is omnipotence; in man, it is will. The seventh note is the first in its ultimate expression. It is power in action, will in motion, omnipotence made manifest. The relatively static centre has become the active sphere, yet the two are one. Within the universe, the seventh is physical material, the sun, the globes and all things evolving upon them. In the Logos, it is the universe; in man, it is the physical body. In manifestation the Spiritual One has become material multiplicity. Because knowledge of the many leads to knowledge of the One, man is placed amongst the manifold expressions of the One, that through knowledge of them he may find and know the One Alone. From the One he goes forth, unconscious of aught save the One, into the many. From the many he returns self-consciously to the One.

The second and the sixth notes, representing respectively Life and its expression, are also paired. Life is all-pervading, omnipresent, the unifying principle of the universe, the Spiritual Sun; its expression is localised as the vital principle in matter, the vitalising principle in Nature and the physical sun. In the universe, the second note is Life; in the Logos, it is omnipresence; in man, it is love; in developed or spiritual man it is wisdom and universal love, from which spring compassion and sefless service. The sixth note in the universe is form, shape, organised matter. In the Logos, it is His " body " of the universe with its heart of fire—the sun—whose life-giving principle appears as roseate fire and, on earth, as an atom of solar vitality. In man, it is one-pointedness; in developed man, it is inspired devotion.

The third and the fifth notes also represent complementary attributes. The third is the interplay between spirit and matter, life and form. The principles governing the manifestation of Spirit and Life through matter and form, the Archetypes of all the resultant forms, truth and the keys of knowledge—all these are connoted by the third. In the universe, the third note is creative energy directed by Universal Mind. In the Logos, it is the passive female principle, the womb in which all forms are conceived and from which all come forth. In man, it is conscience and idealism, morality and truth; in developed man, it appears as comprehension and abstract intelligence, from which spiritual intuitiveness is born. The fifth note is the time expression of that which is everlasting, the progressively developing form of a single Archetype. In the universe, it is the evolving process, growth. In the Logos, it is time. In man, it is the brain and the analytical intelligence; in developed man, it becomes as a crystal lens through which the principles of the third note are projected as Rays and are focussed by it into the brain as illumination, genius and inspiration.

The fourth note is the middle unit, the pivot, the fulcrum, the stable point of rest, the lowest point in the swing of the pendulum of Life between the primordial three pairs of opposites. It is the state of perfect inter-relation, of balance, of the highest art of self-expression, of harmony between Life and form, vehicle and consciousness. It is the point of rest at which the pendulum of manifested Life makes an apparent pause in its everlasting swing between Spirit and matter. In that " momentary pause " of ultimate stability, perfect equipoise, the beauty of the Supreme is revealed. In the universe, it is the beauty of Nature. In the Logos, it is Beauty's Self. In man, it becomes love of the beautiful; in developed man, it is the faculty of perceiving and portraying the beauty of the Supreme.

The essential character of the fourth is darkness, stillness, equipoise, as of creative night before creative dawn. Physical, mental or spiritual germination demands the covering of the mantle of darkness. So also in the production of a work of art, the true artist withdraws his consciousness from the light of day into the darkness of the creative night within himself, into the balanced stillness in which his creation is conceived. The artist-creator in any branch of the arts must have attained equilibrium. This is the law of creation, whether of universe, solar system, planet, man, or human work of art. In this mental stillness is achieved the true vision or insight without which all art is lifeless. Only when the artist has found and entered that state will the fire of genius descend upon him in its full Pentecostal powers.

As the student contemplates each one of the seven, he becomes identified with a seventh part of the Whole and merges his consciousness therein. He thereafter strikes in turn all the seven notes, listens in meditation to each, and in each becomes absorbed. Finally, through each he becomes the Whole, the sevenfold man consciously one with the sevenfold universe. This is the goal. Wise, indeed, is he who by contemplation knows and understands this sevenfold universe—the seven great notes, severally and as a chord. He knows them as the seven keys of Life which open all doors to Truth—Truth which is enshrined within the temple of Nature.

The sevenfold classification is to be traced throughout all the kingdoms of Nature, including the super-human and angelic. In this exposition the Manifestations of the One, the Three and the Seven as human temperament and faculty are chiefly considered, though some information is also offered concerning colour, jewels and other correspondences.

Each Ray is taken in turn and, in the light of Theosophy, suggestions are made concerning its relations to Aspects of the Blessed Trinity, the chief qualities of character and the type of man, the highest and the lowest manifestation, the method of obtaining results by the different Ray types, the defects of character, the corresponding body or principle of man, the colour, the jewel, and the symbol.

As stated later in this book, the pure Ray type is rare, admixtures with consequent modification of ideal, temperament and method being the rule. For purposes of exposition, however, relatively pure Ray types are described. The evolutionary position or "age" of the Spiritual Self usually decides the degree in which the Ray qualities and virtues are displayed and the defects and limitations are overcome. As a general rule, the more advanced the Ego,[1] the more readily discernible in the personality is the primary Ray.

[1] *Ego.* "Self"; the unified triad, Atma-Buddhi-Manas, or the duad [dyad], Atma-Buddhi, that immortal part of man which reincarnates and gradually progresses to the final goal—Nirvana. Also the consciousness in man—"I am I"—or the feeling of "I-am-ship". Esoteric philosophy teaches the existence of two Egos in man, the mortal or personal, and the Higher, the Divine and the Impersonal, calling the former "personality" and the latter "Individuality". Adapted from *The Theosophical Glossary*, H. P. Blavatsky.

CHAPTER II

THE FIRST RAY

THE first Ray corresponds to the First Aspect, God the Father, the Creator. The preponderant qualities of first Ray men are will, power, strength, courage, determination, leadership, independence, dignity rising on occasion to majesty, daring and executive ability. This type of man is the natural ruler and leader, the statesman, the Empire-builder and colonizer, the soldier, the explorer and the pioneer. Alexander the Great was typical of this Ray when he wept for more worlds to conquer. In the early stages of evolution these activities are largely physical. In the later phases they become mental and spiritual. The will is then exerted not so much as personal effort and strain, but in effortless, frictionless expression of the One Will.

The ideal of the Ray is strength, the first Ray man greatly appreciating the presence of this quality, indeed tending to judge the value of all conduct and achievement according to the measure of strength employed. He fights to the end and is able to condone almost any act if the quality of strength shines through it. He finds it difficult to tolerate weakness in any form and tends to despise those who give in. For him God, or the highest good, is the Principle of Power in all things. The greatest evils are weakness and surrender. The driving impulse is to attain and to conquer and such men are often seen at their best in adversity. The highest attainment is victory and the greatest interior experience comes from the exhilaration of power, kingship, dominion.

The most natural first Ray method of obtaining results is to evoke from within oneself great will-power, to become charged with the determination to succeed at all costs, refusing to consider the possibility of defeat. Heedless of fatigue up to the point of utter exhaustion, the first Ray man exerts great mental and physical pressure upon himself and others and, when necessary, ruthlessly overrides or destroys all barriers and obstacles. As a teacher, he accentuates self-reliance, both in the attainment of knowledge and as a way of life. He is forceful in driving home the truths to be taught and leaves pupils to stand alone as far as possible.

The apotheosis is omnipotence, or to become consciously one with the divine Will; for as he ascends the spiritual heights he must renounce the individual for the divine Will. The immediate purpose of all human life is spiritual, intellectual and physical evolution to the stature of the perfect man, and the ultimate objective of first Ray man is to fulfil a high office in the spiritual direction of the life of nations, planets and solar systems. Each life is therefore a training and a preparation for offices to be held in the future. Man's passage through phases of ignorance, impotence,

transgression and consequent suffering to the attainment
of wisdom, power and unbroken happiness and peace,
would seem to be indicated in Tennyson's words:

> " Act first, this Earth, a stage so gloom'd with
>   woe,
>   You all but sicken at the shifting scenes.
> And yet be patient. Our Playwright may
>   show
>   In some fifth Act what this wild Drama
>   means."

In this work, a list of defects displayed in the earlier
stages of evolution by members of each of the seven
Ray types is presented, but without the slightest in-
gredient of judgment and with no thought of adverse
criticism and denunciation. The human race is as yet
but a little more than half way through its evolutionary
development on this planet. Whilst magnificent qualities and great virtues are already displayed, it is
inevitable that their opposites should also be apparent.
Amongst the defects of the first Ray displayed in the
earlier stages of evolution are ruthlessness, hardness,
stubbornness, pride, superciliousness, unadaptability,
being ready to work only on lines which appeal
personally, indifference to and even scorn of the
opinions, rights and feelings of others, tyranny, thirst
for power, egotism, braggadocio, extravagance, aggres-
siveness, wilfulness, assumption of superiority, individualism, mental rigidity and making final pronounce-
ments upon debatable subjects, thereby closing

2

discussion and prohibiting freedom of enquiry. Dogma, or a supposedly authoritative statement, sometimes without regard to inherent truth or reasonableness, is used as a bludgeon to stun into silence enquiring minds. Recognition of the importance of authority in the maintenance of order can cause first Ray people to use both personal position and dogma to forbid further investigation. This is done, whether consciously or unconsciously, to crush opposition and restore personal prestige and dominance.

The greatest suffering can be experienced in defeat, degradation from office, displacement, humiliation, subordination and exile.

Of the seven principles of man,[1] that of Spiritual Will or *Atma*[2] influences the character and conduct of first Ray man. The corresponding colour in the spectrum, generally present in the aura, is white tinged with electric blue at Egoic levels and bright vermillion in the personal aura. The jewel is the diamond and the symbol is that of the First Aspect of the Logos, the Creator, the "One Alone", the circle with a point in the centre. Of the arts, dancing represents the first Ray and those in whom that Ray predominates,

[1] Vide *The Self and its Sheaths* and *The Seven Principles of Man*, Annie Besant. These are variously indicated, one list being: Spiritual Will, Spiritual Wisdom, Spiritual Intelligence, the antahkarana or bridge, mental, emotional and physical. This classification is used throughout this work.

[2] *Atma*. The seventh Principle of man, the highest expression in him of the divine Monad. The innermost essence of universe and man. Adapted from *The Secret Doctrine* and *The Theosophical Glossary*, H.P. Blavatsky.

whether practising the art or not, will be more likely to respond to and be influenced by dancing than by other branches of the arts. This Ray choice of artistic medium and method would appear to be true for all Rays.

Amongst world religions, Hinduism displays the characteristics of the first Ray. In Hindu scriptures, God, in one Aspect, is represented as a Divine Dancer and the creation, preservation and regeneration of the universe as a continuous Cosmic dance. The first Ray predominates in the doctrine and ethics of Hinduism and the seventh in its ceremonies and *mantras*.[1] The evocation and transmission of spiritual power, and the insistence upon a high code of ethics or *dharma* as summed up in the Golden Rule enunciated in the *Laws of Manu*[2], represent the influence and action of the first Ray.

If a chart of the seven Rays be folded, using the fourth as a hinge, the horizontal columns of the first and seventh Rays will come into contact with each other and the natural correspondences between the Rays will be revealed. The seventh Ray may be regarded as a manifestation in form of the first, or as representing power in action. Christ displayed to perfection the qualities of these two Rays when by virtue of His power and His knowledge He stilled the tempest with the words " Peace be still ",[3] as also in

[1] *Mantras.* Scientifically chosen and arranged words and sentences of power which, when chanted, liberate potent energies.

[2] *Manu.* The great Indian legislator, almost a Divine Being. *The Theosophical Glossary*, H. P. Blavatsky.

[3] *Mark* IV, 39.

all of His production of supernormal phenomena, mis-called miracles.   King Arthur represents the Christ in His first Ray aspect as Spiritual King.

The first Ray qualities are represented in the characters, words and actions of many well-known leaders of men.   Here are some examples:

HANDS DOWN

" One night back in the '20's, when General Mac-Arthur was Superintendent of West Point, he and a second lieutenant were motoring back from New York to the Military Academy.   On a lonely stretch of road, two masked bandits stopped the car.   With a flourish of pistols they opened the door, ordered hands up.   Instinc-tively, the lieutenant upped his hands, but was amazed to see MacArthur sitting quietly, arms folded across his chest.   ' Up with them! ' growled the thug ominously.

" MacArthur didn't budge.   ' I'm a brigadier general in the United States Army,' he drawled, ' and no one can force me to put up my hands! ' The bandit, his confidence obviously shattered, lowered his gun un-certainly; then, without a word, backed out and slammed the door."—Mary Van Rensselaer Thayer in *Washington Post.*

In his War Memoirs, Winston Churchill writes interestingly of the right use of political power:

" In my long political experience, I had held most of the great offices of State, but I readily admit that the post which had now fallen to me was the one I liked the best.   Power, for the sake of lording it over fellow-creatures or adding to personal pomp, is rightly judged base. But power in a national crisis, when a man believes he knows what orders should be given, is a blessing.

"In any sphere of action there can be no comparison between the positions of number one and numbers two, three or four. The duties and the problems of all persons other than number one are quite different, and in many ways more difficult.

"It is always a misfortune when number two or three has to initiate a dominant plan or policy. He has to consider not only the merits of the policy, but the mind of his chief; not only what to advise, but what it is proper for him in his station to advise; not only what to do, but how to get it agreed, and how to get it done. Moreover, numbers two or three will have to reckon with numbers four, five and six, or may be some bright outsider, number 20.

"Ambition, not so much for vulgar ends, but for fame, glints in every mind. There are always several points of view which may be right, and many which are plausible. I was ruined for the time being in 1915 over the Dardanelles, and a supreme enterprise was cast away, through my trying to carry out a major and cardinal operation of war from a subordinate position. Men are ill-advised to try such ventures. This lesson had sunk into my nature."

The quality of fighting to the end, characteristic of the first Ray, is revealed in Winston Churchill's famous words, uttered when the fortunes of Britain were at their lowest in the early phases of the Second World War:

" Even though large tracts of Europe and many old and famous States have fallen or may fall into the grip of the Gestapo and all the odious apparatus of Nazi rule, we shall not flag or fail. We shall go on to the end. We shall fight in France, we shall fight in the sea and oceans, we shall fight with growing confidence and growing strength in the air; we shall defend our Island, whatever the cost may be. We shall fight on the beaches, we shall fight on the landing-grounds, we shall fight in the fields and in the streets, we shall fight in the hills; we shall never surrender; and even if, which I do not for a moment believe, this Island or a large part of it were subjugated and starving, then our Empire beyond the seas, armed and guarded by the British Fleet, would carry on the struggle, until, in God's good time, the New World, with all its power and might, steps forth to the rescue and the liberation of the Old."

Scott, the Antarctic Explorer, was described as " an indefeatable sportsman, buoyant, indomitable". Dr. Wilson's advice to Oates when his feet were becoming useless, " Slog on, just slog on", and the gallant action of the latter in walking out into the blizzard to his death rather than become a more serious burden to his comrades are typical of the first Ray, as is the explorer's ideal: " To strive, to seek, to find and not to yield ".[1] Of Shackleton it was written: " When you

[1] Tennyson's *Ulysses*.

are in a hopeless position, when there seems no way out, get down on your knees and pray for Shackleton."

Time for January the 10th, 1949, reported words and acts of General George Patton which exemplify the first Ray type of man:

" Like many another military man, the late General George Patton was prayerful as well as profane. He was also a peremptory commander who did not hesitate to let the Almighty know what kind of co-operation he expected. When bad weather held up his advance before the Battle of the Bulge, he is reported (by one of his staff) to have called in Third Army Chaplain James H. O'Neill, and said: ' Chaplain, I want you to publish a prayer for good weather . . . . See if we can't get God to work on our side.' The chaplain demurred but Patton roared: ' Chaplain, are you teaching me theology or are you the chaplain of the Third Army? I want a prayer.' The prayer, printed with a Christmas greeting, was distributed to the troops."

First Ray attributes displayed by King George V are revealed in the book, *King George V, His Life and Reign* by Sir Harold Nicolson. Amongst the many great qualities of the late King George V was the tendency to direct his family like a ship's company of which he was the master and martinet. His children were greatly afraid of him and tended to agree with everything he said. When the Duke of York (later George VI) married Lady Elizabeth Bowes-Lyon, his father wrote to him: " You have always been so sensible, and ready to listen to any advice and to agree with my opinions about people and things, that I feel that we have always got on well together." Here is displayed the first Ray habit of measuring the value of people according to the degree in which they listen to their advice and agree with their opinions.

CHAPTER III

THE SECOND RAY

THE second Ray corresponds to the Second Aspect of the Blessed Trinity, God the Son, the Preserver. The special qualities of the Ray are wisdom, love, intuition, insight, philanthropy, a sense of unity, spiritual sympathy, compassion, loyalty and generosity. The type of man is the sage, the philanthropist, the reformer, the teacher, the inspirer, the humanitarian, the healer and the servant of men, imbued with a universal love which often overflows to the lower kingdoms of Nature. Froebel, the great educationalist and reformer of the last century, who coined the word "kindergarten", and Madame Montessori, are splendid examples of second Ray educators, though both of them display in a high degree the qualities of other Rays.

The ideal of second Ray man is impersonal, universal love founded upon recognition of the unity of life. When highly evolved, he is intuitive and aspires to radiate upon the world, without thought of return or reward, wisdom and love which will uplift and inspire all whom they reach. He also becomes moved to develop to their highest degree as positive powers

the spirit of service and the qualities of purity, refine-
ment, gentleness, tenderness, charity, goodwill, bene-
volence, harmony and protectiveness.   Loyalty in both
friendship and love is one of his greatest virtues,
friendship being a veritable religion, and loyalty, especially in the face of failure and disloyalty, its highest
expression.   The phrase, " Love is not love which
alters when it alteration finds", partly expresses the
second Ray ideal of love.

For the second Ray man, God is the Principle of
Wisdom, of universal, radiant love and of self-sacrifice.
He sees the divine creative act as a continuous,
voluntary and sacramental sacrifice in which God
perpetually surrenders His life that all may live.   He
judges all conduct and achievement according to the
measure in which they are founded upon and display
these qualities.   He is able to forgive even evil conduct if motived by love.   This is well stated in the
words:

" Those who walk in love may wander far,

But God will bring them where the blessed
are."

Indeed, when well developed he is able always to love,
and so to forgive, the sinner, even whilst denouncing
and combating the sin.   The greatest evils for this type
are hatred, separateness, selfishness, cruelty and disloyalty.   The driving impulse is to save, to teach, to
serve, to heal, to share, to give happiness and to create
and maintain harmony.   The highest attainment for
second Ray people is the full realisation and expression

in conduct of unity. To extend the range of such realisation and expression is their supreme preoccupation. They aspire also successfully to impart wisdom, to illumine others from within.

The second Ray man does not seek to overcome, override or crush enemies by superior force; he prefers to dissipate their enmity, which he feels acutely, to change it when possible into co-operation, to win their sympathy and to turn them into friends. He exercises intuitive insight and perception and seeks self-illumination when in the presence of enmity or obstruction. Non-resistance and turning the other cheek are natural to him and his method of fighting is rather to wrestle with the opponent than to strike him down. He is also very ready to negotiate and prefers an agreed to an enforced solution.

As teacher, he freely shares all knowledge which can be helpful, accentuates the value of self-illumination from within, encourages the use of the intuition and bestows happiness. The qualifications, personal nature and motive of the teacher are regarded as of great significance, the profession ideally having been chosen as a true vocation rather than a means of livelihood alone. He warns againts confusing education with training in which memory and imitation are accentuated. He constantly seeks to wake the inherent capacities of his pupils, especially the urge to produce that which is beautiful.

He believes in the provision of interest and a sufficiency of permissible activities into which the boundless energy welling up in the child, for example, can flow without restriction or so-called naughtiness. Psychological integration is regarded as an essential part of the process of education.

The following definitions of the functions of education exemplify the second Ray approach:

Spencer: " For complete living."

Aristotle: " For happiness and usefulness."

Ruskin: " Education is not teaching people to know what they do not know, but teaching them to behave as they do not behave."

Tennyson: " Self-reverence, Self-knowledge, Self-control;

These three alone lead Life to Sovereign power." (*Oenone.*)

To these educational ideals might be added:

To help the Inner Self to achieve the fullest self-expression; to produce enlightened citizens; to produce workers for world welfare, high-minded servants of their fellow men.

The Sympathy School in England exemplifies very beautifully one of the teaching methods typical of the second Ray. At this School, in the course of the term every child has one blind day, one lame day, one deaf day, one day when he cannot speak.

The night before the blind day his eyes are bandaged. He awakes blind. He needs help, and the other children lead him about. Through this method he gets a grasp of what it is really like to be blind. And those who help, having been " blind " themselves, are able to guide and direct the blind with understanding.

For the second Ray man his apotheosis is omnipresence, which means to be consciously self-identified with the divine Life in all Nature and in all beings, and so mystically present wherever that Life is manifest. Christ and the Lord Buddha are the great Exemplars of this perfection, portrayed in the words of the Christ:

" Inasmuch as ye have done it unto one of the least of these My brethren, ye have done it unto Me." (*Matt.* XXV. 40.)

" Neither do I condemn thee." (*John* VIII. 11.)

" He that is without sin among you, let him first cast a stone." (*John* VIII. 7.)

" Where two or three are gathered together in My name, there am I in the midst of them." (*Matt.* XVIII. 20.)

" Love your enemies." (*Matt.* V. 44, *Luke* VI. 27, 35.)

" Pray for them which despitefully use you." (*Matt.* V. 44)

" Father forgive them for they know not what they do." (*Luke* XXIII. 34.)

Amongst the defects of the type are sentimentality and sensuality, self-righteousness, hyper-sensitivity, self-pity despendency, the habit of brooding upon and nursing grievances, and difficulty in forgiving sins against the second Ray code. Judgment is often in danger of being obscured by the emotions, especially those of compassion and love. The quality of sympathy, which is characteristic of this Ray, shone out in the words of a young daughter who appealed to her mother for clemency when an older child was being severely reproved: " Mother, please do not be cross with Mary. It makes the room go dark." Second Ray people are prone to impracticability and to immense self-sacrifice for others, sometimes undermining the self-reliance and increasing the selfishness of those on whose behalf such sacrifices are made. They are inclined to over-accentuate the life side of their work to the neglect of the necessity for an equal perfection of form.

The greatest suffering can come from heart-break, discordance in close human relationships, broken faith and trust, misjudgment, coldness, isolation and exclusion, loneliness and neglect.

The principle of man corresponding to the second Ray is that of Wisdom and spiritual intuitiveness or *Buddhi*,[1] the vehicle of the Christ Consciousness. The colours are golden yellow and azure blue. The jewel is the sapphire and the symbol is the Latin cross. Of the arts, music with its harmonizing influence represents this Ray.

Buddhism, as its name suggests, is predominantly a second Ray religion. The doctrinal, theological (where

---

[1] *Buddhi*. The sixth Principle of man, the vehicle of *Atma* expressed as wisdom and spiritual intuitiveness. Adapted from *The Theosophical Glossary* and *The Secret Doctrine*, H. P. Blavatsky.

the theology is founded upon truth), redemptive, saving and teaching aspects of all World Faiths represent the second Ray influence in them.

The Ray correspondence is with the sixth Ray, through which is manifested more individually and emotionally the universal love and capacity for self-sacrifice and self-surrender in devotion to a leader and a cause typical of the second Ray.

The Lord Christ, in His perfect wisdom, His universal love and His boundless compassion, tenderness and pity for all that lives, especially for all that suffers, is a great Exemplar of the qualities of the second Ray.

CHAPTER IV

THE THIRD RAY

THE third Ray is a manifestation of the Third Aspect of the Blessed Trinity, the Holy Ghost, the Regenerator and Transformer.

The qualities of character are comprehension—especially of fundamental principles—understanding, a deeply penetrative and interpretative mind, adaptability, tact, dignity, the sense of which is very strong, and recognition of the power and value of silence. Capacity for creative ideation is one of the characteristic powers. The types of men are the philosopher, the organiser, the diplomat, the strategist, the tactician, the scholar, the economist, the banker, the chess player, the judge, the allegorist, the interpreter and the cartoonist. Leaders such as Churchill, Roosevelt, Stalin, Montgomery, Rommel, Smuts, are outstanding examples of men in whom the first and third Rays are highly developed.

Full comprehension is the ideal, God being regarded chiefly as the Principle of Truth. Untruth, intellectual obtuseness and lack of comprehension are the greatest evils. The driving impulse is wholly and impersonally to grasp all the fundamental principles and factors of a subject and to combine and apply them to its perfect comprehension and application. The highest attainment is the full and perfect perception of truth and genius partly arising from an overflow of contemplation.

Unlike either the first or second Ray types, in obtaining results the third Ray man tends to withdraw mentally, as does the hermit physically, from the problem or obstacle into the realm of abstract thought, there to ponder and meditate until complete enlightenment occurs. Comprehension and synthesis of all the factors involved is thus gained and as a result the solution of the problem is perceived. In his own life he learns to "burn up *karma* [1] in the fire of knowledge" and

---

[1] *Karma.* The Law of Causation, Balance, Compensation, by which every action begets a reaction; the actor becomes the attractor for a similar action. "Physically, action; metaphysically, the Law of Retribution, the Law of cause and effect or Ethical Causation. Nemesis, only in one sense, that of bad Karma. It is the eleventh Nidana in the concatenation of causes and effects in orthodox Buddhism; yet it is the power that controls all things, the resultant of moral action, the metaphysical Samskara, or the moral effect of an act committed for the attainment of something which gratifies a personal desire. There is the Karma of merit and the Karma of demerit. Karma neither punishes nor rewards; it is simply the one Universal Law which guides unerringly, and, so to say, blindly, all other laws productive of certain effects along the grooves of their respective causations. When Buddhism teaches that 'Karma is that moral kernel (of any being) which alone survives death and continues in transmigration or reincarnation', it simply means that there remains naught after each Personality but the causes produced by it; causes which are undying, *i.e.* which cannot be eliminated from the Universe until replaced by their legitimate effects, and wiped out by them, so to speak, and such causes — unless compensated during the life of the person who produced them with adequate effects, will follow the reincarnated Ego, and reach it in its subsequent reincarnation until a harmony between effects and causes is fully re-established." *The Theosophical Glossary,* H.P. Blavatsky.

Vide *Reincarnation, Fact or Fallacy?* Geoffrey Hodson.

discovers and applies the principles of that spiritual alchemy by which adversity is changed into happiness, and all that is base in human nature is transmuted into wisdom and power.   As scientist he would be alchemist as well as chemist, astrologer as well as astronomer, and metaphysician as well as physicist and mathematician.   He achieves results by means of prolonged, sequential thinking and a perfection of both strategy and tactics.   He skilfully employs the method of the trap and the net, being ready to use any appropriate method without regard for personal inclination.   As teacher, he explains principles, encouraging the pupils to work out their application by their own mental efforts, often leaving gaps and even permitting perplexity in order to evoke enquiry and inspire to research.   Impersonality in the approach to truth is inculcated.

This type feels greatly the necessity for complete comprehension in all the affairs of life, responds far less to an imposed ethical code than to interior realisation of the valid reasons for particular kinds of conduct.   He learns also to interpret and use circumstances as guides to conduct and wisely to wait upon the logic of events.   In the intellectual skill and wisdom with which the Lord Christ defeated those who sought to entrap Him, notably in the question of the payment of tribute money and of the woman taken in adultery, as also in His silence when accused, (if one may presume to say so) the qualities of the third Ray were displayed to a high degree. The phrase " Give me understanding,

and I shall keep Thy law "[1] perfectly expresses
the point of view of this Ray, the apotheosis of which
is omniscience through unity with the Major Mind.

Amongst the defects of the type are coldness, individualism, selfishness, indecision through seeing too
many sides, aloofness, intrigue, cruelty, unreadiness
openly to adopt a cause, failure to support in a crisis, de-
liberately and unscrupulously to deceive as did the Nazi
Minister for Propaganda, Goebbels, insincerity, cunning
and too great attention to form, detail and system to
the neglect of the spirit and the larger purposes of life.

Inversely, there is sometimes a proneness to live too
much in the realm of principles, long range plans,
schemes and ideals and consequently to become im-
practical and remote from the world.

The insincerity of which third Ray people are capable
is well described in the words of a modern Dictator, who
is reported (*Time*, February 14th, 1949) to have written:
" A diplomat's words must have no relation to actions
—otherwise what kind of diplomat is he? Good words
are a mask for the concealment of bad deeds. Sincere
diplomats are no more possible than dry water or
wooden iron."

Of the late Field-Marshal Smuts it was written:
" During the early days of his premiership in the
Union of South Africa, General Smuts planned to make
a speech to the Parliament. He called his secretary
and said: ' Go to the library and get me some statistical
data to illustrate some of the points I want to make.'

[1] *Psalms* CXIX, 34.

" The secretary came back seven hours later and said: ' General, there is no man alive who could get that information in less than five years! '

" The next day the General got up and made an eloquent speech. He drove home every point with a multiplicity of statistical detail. Everyone was enormously impressed, but no one so much as his secretary. When the General retired to his office the secretary asked: ' Where did you get all those wonderful statistics? '

" And General Smuts said: ' Well, you told me no man alive could compile them in less than five years. So I made a few rough estimates and I figured it would take at least that long for anyone to check up on me! ' " (Merryle Stanely Rukeyser.)

The greatest suffering can be experienced when proven incompetent and in error, when plunged into intellectual darkness and defeat and from deprivation of dignity, including " loss of face ".

The principle of man is that of abstract intelligence or Higher *Manas*,[1] *Causal Body* [2] or the vehicle of the

---

[1] *Manas*. " The mind ", the mental faculty which makes of man an intelligent and moral being, and distinguishes him from the animal; a synonym of Mahat. Esoterically, however, it means, when unqualified, the Higher Ego, or the sentient reincarnating Principle in man. When qualified it is called by Theosophists Buddhi-Manas or the spiritual Soul in contradistinction to its human reflection—Kama-Manas. *The Theosophical Glossary*, H. P. Blavatsky. Regarded in this book as the conjoined fifth and fourth principles of man, vehicles of his abstract and concrete mentality.

[2] *Causal Body*. The vehicle and expression at the level of abstract intellect of the incarnating Entity or Ego. The body of intelligence or understanding.

human Ego. The colour is emerald green, the jewel the emerald, the Ray correspondence is with the fifth Ray, that of the concrete mind, and the symbol is the triangle. Whilst the third Ray man would be intellectually concerned with the great principles of life, with philosophy and metaphysics, the fifth Ray man would more readily pursue detailed scientific knowledge and seek to apply the results to physical life. Of the Arts, poetry, which is mental music, the perfect language, represents the third Ray.

The Chaldean religion, with its astrological basis and practice, is predominantly third Ray. The philosophical and metaphysical aspects of all World Faiths represent the third Ray influence in them.

Amongst explorers, Scott was extolled for scientific leadership and Amunsden for swift and efficient travel, these references to their organising powers indicating third Ray development. All great war Leaders must in modern days be imbued, not only with the fighting qualities of the first Ray, but also with the strategical and organising abilities of the third. Field-Marshal Montgomery exemplified this in his careful, precise preparations, his predilection for ensuring the availability of all forces and supplies necessary for victory before starting, including control of the air, his close study of the opponent's character (during the Desert Campaign he kept a portrait of Rommel in his caravan), his readiness to deceive by a feint, and, when necessary, quickly to revise the whole scheme (as when attacking the Mareth Line), his location of the right divisions in the right places at the right time, his complete self-confidence and his delivery of a murderous blow with every available weapon.

The motto of the Cavendish family, " Cavendo tutus", meaning " Secure by caution ", exemplifies the third Ray, as does the following story:

A Catholic priest displayed the tactical skill and ready adaptability of the third Ray in the following story related by Paul Marcus:

" Among the guests at a dinner my parents gave recently were a rabbi and a Catholic priest. When the party sat down to dinner, they were confronted with one of those seemingly insurmountable moments —who was going to say grace? Everyone looked meekly down at his plate; my mother and father gulped for words. At the crest of the terrible moment, the priest looked around the table and said: " If you don't mind, I'd like to say an old Jewish prayer."

" They all bowed their heads, and the priest said grace—in Hebrew."

CHAPTER V

THE FOURTH RAY

THE fourth Ray, together with the third, fifth, sixth and seventh, is said to be a manifestation of the Third Aspect of the Blessed Trinity. Its qualities are creative ideation, harmony, balance, beauty and rhythm. The special faculty of the fourth Ray man is the power to perceive and portray, both through the Arts and through life, the " principle of beauty in all things ".[1] He generally displays great versatility and sometimes the gift of mimicry. Even whilst not yet possessing them, he is able to display—one might almost say simulate—the qualities of all the Rays. He has a strong sense of form, symmetry, equilibrium and a sensitive taste for all that is beautiful in the Arts, in Nature and in life.

The type of man is the artist for whom God, or the highest good, is the principle of Beauty in the Universe, ugliness being regarded as the greatest evil. The mode of artistic expression and the choice of medium are influenced by the dominant sub-Ray. The driving impulse is to release the influence of beauty upon the world, to mediate between the realms of pure beauty

[1] Keats.

and those of its imperfect expression, the Arts serving as links between the two. Those orators possessed of the art of rhythmic speech, capable of charming, persuading, captivating and carrying away an audience, the true spell-binders, display the quality of the fourth Ray.

The fourth Ray standard and test of human beings, nations and civilisations is far more that of beauty than of temporal power, possessions, armaments and financial standing. Some artists can condone all conduct through which the light of beauty shines and are unable to forgive ugliness. They feel acutely the need for the presence of harmony and beauty in their surroundings and can suffer greatly from their absence.

The fourth Ray man obtains his results by markedly individual methods, success depending upon perfection of technique, whether in the Arts or in life. He is a natural mediator and interpreter. His apotheosis is to become a master artist, a genius in every Art, especially that of living, which for him includes full self-expression and the maintenance of perfect relationships. Evidence exists that the branch of the Arts chosen by those in whom the fourth Ray predominates may vary in successive lives, under the influence of a sub-Ray. They perceive and seek to portray in every thought, word and deed the divine Beauty which shines throughout the universe. They achieve their results by dramatisation, illustration and by the appeal of beauty, rhythm, perfection and charm, the means employed being enchantment and allurement. As teachers they illustrate and dramatize.

Amongst the defects in the fourth Ray are instability, restlessness, vacillation, sensuousness, posing, self-conceit, self-indulgence, improvidence, cynicism concerning those more successful than themselves and a sense of superiority over less gifted individuals. They suffer alternation of moods. They can be elevated to lofty exaltation and cast down into depression and despair.

" Every artist knows, and dreads, the converse pause of despondency that follows upon achievement. The greater the enthusiasm, the more deadly the rebound." [1]

" A passionate mood is a concentration of experience, a hurrying together of thoughtful moments. Emotion is thought in a hurry. This speeding-up can only come at a time of unusual fullness of suggestion, spontaneously; and is followed by exhaustion and disappointment; for it cannot be sustained." [2]

Fourth Ray people may also display a tendency to daydream, to live in a world of fantasy. Unless the will-force of the first Ray is active in them, they experience vague yearnings for great things and yet fail of accomplishment. The greatest suffering is generally due to frustration and failure to achieve perfect self-expression.

The principle of man is the bridge between the Higher Self and the lower, the *antahkarana*.[3] This

---

[1] *The Mind and Work of Charles Sims*, by Alan Sims.

[2] *Picture Making*, by Charles Sims, R.A.

[3] *Antahkarana*, Sanskrit. Antar=middle or interior, and karana= cause, instrument. Technically used to refer to the bridge between the Higher and the Lower Minds, the internal instrument operative between them.

principle " serves as a medium of communication between the two, and conveys from the lower to the
Higher Ego all those personal impressions and thoughts
of man which can, by their nature, be assimilated and
stored by the undying Entity, and be thus made
immortal with it, these being the only elements of the
evanescent Personality that survive death and time ".[1]
The mission of the artist would thus appear to be, by
means of beauty, to elevate the consciousness of man
into realisation of the beauty and the splendour of
Nature and of God. Thus the truly great artist serves
as priest and mediator between God and man.

The colour is a tawny bronze, the jewel is the jasper
and the symbol is the square and compasses associated
with Freemasonry. The fourth Ray may be regarded
as a lens through which the lights of all the Rays
are focussed. Of the Arts, opera represents the fourth
Ray, being a synthesis of various branches of Art.

The Orphic religion, with its keynote of Beauty,
was predominantly fourth Ray, which also finds
expression in every tendency towards colourful appur-
tenances and adornments and the use of the Arts in
religious worship.

The following verses and lines express the artist's
view of life:

        " For I have seen
    In lonely places, and in lonelier hours
    My vision of the rainbow-aureoled face
    Of Her whom men call Beauty; proud, austere;

[1] *The Theosophical Glossary*, H. P. Blavatsky.

Dim vision of the flawless, perfect face,
Divinely fugitive, that haunts the world
And lifts men's spiral thoughts to lovelier dream."

"O world as God has made it! All is beauty."
                                        Browning.

"There is no light but Thine; with Thee all
beauty glows."   Rev. John Keble.

"Beauty is truth, truth beauty,—that is all
Ye know on earth and all ye need to know."
                          Keats, *Ode on a Grecian Urn.*

"Take away from our hearts that love of the
beautiful, and you take away all the charm of
life."   Rousseau.

"I have always believed that God is only beauty
put into action."   Rousseau.

"The best part of Beauty is what a picture cannot
express."   Bacon.

"Beauty itself doth persuade the eyes of men without an orator."   Shakespeare.

CHAPTER VI

THE FIFTH RAY

THE special qualities of the fifth Ray are those typical of the analytical, deductive, formal mind, the whole interest and ideal of people of this Ray being the acquirement and, where the second Ray is also well developed, the dissemination of factual knowledge. In this pursuit, those in whom the fifth Ray is very dominant are capable of displaying unwearying patience and the extreme of thoroughness and method, particularly in the repeated examination and the classification of intricate and minute details.

The type of man is the scientist, the mathematician, the lawyer and detective. In the early stages of development the chief interest is in physical science, this being later extended into the domain of the occult and the metaphysical.

The fifth Ray mind is brilliant, flashing, swift, witty, technical, analytical, accurate, positive, and possesses great capacity for specialisation and grasp of detail. As ideals it prizes highly truth, mental detachment and accuracy of observation, of deduction and of exposition. God is regarded as the principle of Truth, and untruth, ignorance, inaccuracy and a biassed mind are the greatest evils.

The driving impulse of fifth Ray man is to discover knowledge, to reach truth. This, however, must be demonstrable, as for example, by correct prediction, based upon acquired data. He obtains his results by means of the brilliant and patient use of the mind. He thinks, seeks, searches, probes, experiments, patiently observes and calculates and then makes accurate deductions from his discoveries. He uses his mind like an auger to bore to the heart of problems, always adhering to the scientific method. This is described by Anton J. Carlson as "rechecked observations and experiments, objectively recorded with absolute honesty and without fear or favour". This preoccupation sometimes tends to make his mind so inelastic and his methods so rigid and unadaptable that full achievement is denied him. When, however, the third Ray aspect of his nature, with its characteristics of adaptability and philosophic thought, begins to influence his concrete mind, as would seem to be occurring in the case of many modern scientists, this, combined with the magnificent qualities already referred to, ensures his success as a great discoverer and revealer of knowledge to man. As a teacher, he elucidates logically and fully, fills in details, uses diagrams and inculcates accuracy.

The apotheosis is to become a master scientist, a genius of intellect in every branch of science, physical and super-physical, success in the latter field, and sometimes in the former, leading to the exhilaration of mental mastery. With his brother of the third Ray, he ultimately becomes one with the Major Mind, and so attains perfection both in knowledge itself and in the practical application of the scientific principles upon which the Universe is founded.

Amongst the defects are separateness, emotional coldness, destructive criticism, mental rigidity and one-track-mindedness, a tendency to perceive and unduly accentuate the faults in others, iconoclasm which is not supplemented by readiness or ability to construct, wounding by telling " your faults for your own good " and being too unfeeling to soften the blow or endeavour to be tactful, pleasure in "pricking bubbles " (often a useful if disconcerting function), inability to " suffer fools gladly", intolerance of everything emotional, mystical and intuitional, scepticism, materialism and pride. Other faults are self-centredness, smallness of vision, prying curiosity and inquisitiveness, meanness demanding a *quid pro quo*, becoming excessively pedantic and accentuating form to the neglect of life. On occasion this type displays an almost childlike lack of wisdom and effectiveness in the conduct of life, sometimes due, perhaps, to proverbial absent-mindedness.

In religion, where this is accepted, the fifth Ray man is inclined to be dogmatic and curiously unreasoning. In excessive preoccupation with tradition, dogma, doctrine, creed and form, he not infrequently loses sight of the inner life and of the necessity for interior experience and enlightenment. This type is frequently very selfish and acquisitive and, unless the character is modified by the presence of the qualities of other Rays, notably the second, third and sixth, tends to keep its discoveries and possessions to itself, *e.g.* to patent inventions. The developed second or sixth Ray man, on the other hand, delights to share all discoveries and gifts, world welfare being the motive for all research and all endeavour. The complete reliance of the spiritually unawakened fifth Ray man upon analytical processes and demonstrable proof is inclined to render him somewhat blind to the great principles behind manifestation and impervious to inspiration and intuition.

The greatest suffering can be experienced when proven at fault and especially when, proven in error, he is made the subject of ridicule or scorn. Such mental defeat and dishonour deeply wound the nature of fifth Ray man.

The more active and most used principle of this type of man is the mental body or lower *Manas*. The colour is lemon-yellow, the jewel the topaz and the symbol the five-pointed star. The fifth Ray is in correspondence with the third, of the qualities and attainments of which it is the concrete expression. Ultimately the two are blended into a single instrument of consciousness, displaying the highest qualities of both of the vehicles and both of the Rays. Of the Arts, painting represents the fifth Ray.

The Egyptian religion, with the Hermetic philosophy as its heart and its key-note of Truth, was predominantly fifth Ray, as is the scholastic aspect of every World Faith.

The vivid deductions of Sherlock Holmes, as also of all other detectives, and the cold, precise reasoning of the legal mind, are all examples of the activity of the formal mind which is generally accentuated in fifth Ray man.

The story is told of President Abraham Lincoln that, travelling in a train with a friend, his attention was drawn to some sheep in a field. " Those sheep " said the friend, " have been newly shorn ". Looking out, Lincoln said, " On this side ".

CHAPTER VII

THE SIXTH RAY

THE special qualities of the sixth Ray are sacrificial love, burning enthusiasm for a cause, fiery ardour, one-pointedness, single-mindedness, selfless devotion, adoration, an intense sympathy for the sufferings of others even to the extent of reproducing them as in the stigmata, idealism expressed as practical service, and loyalty, " the marrow of honour " (Von Hindenburg). The type of man is the mystic, the devotee, the saint, the active philanthropist, the martyr, the evangelist, the missionary and the reformer. Examples are Brother Lawrence, St. Francis, St. Clare, St. Teresa (third and sixth Rays) and General Booth (sixth and first Rays).

The ideal is complete self-consecration, self-sacrifice even unto death for an ideal, a cause or a leader. Selfless service in relief of the sufferings of the world, most keenly felt, is the driving impulse behind the life of the developed sixth Ray man, for whom God is the principle of Self-Sacrifice, Love and Goodness. Whether as soldier, lover, philosopher or scientist, to this ideal he is " faithful unto death ". Selfishness, individualism,

4

divided loyalty, disloyalty, betrayal of individual and of public trust, and hate are the greatest evils.

The sixth Ray person obtains his results by the extreme of one-pointedness; he carries his devotion to such lofty heights that he loses himself in his ideal, becomes its veritable incarnation. In the fire of his enthusiasm, he burns up both the defects of his own character and the outer obstacles which stand in the way of the fulfilment of his ideal. As teacher he inspires, enfires and, amongst other qualities, evokes hero-worship and loyalty in his pupils. The apotheosis is selfless and perfect service of the will of God.

Amongst the defects of the type are emotionalism, sensuality, fanaticism, obsession, susceptibility to glamour, intolerance and the extreme of blind hero-worship. Acute suffering is caused by the disloyalty of loved and trusted friends and by being misunderstood and misjudged, particularly as to motives.

The principle of man is the *astral body*,[1] the colour roseate fire. The jewel is the ruby and the symbol the rose of four petals in the form of an equal-armed cross. The correspondence is with the second Ray, of many of the qualities of which the sixth Ray is an active expression. Amongst the Arts, architecture—frozen music—represents the sixth Ray.

The Christian religion, especially in its devotional and mystical aspects, is predominantly sixth Ray. The

---

[1] *Astral Body*. The vehicle of human emotions built of the first type of matter more subtle than physical ether, denominated astral because self-radiant.

seventh Ray is, however, well represented in its ceremonial forms of worship, perhaps reaching its culmination in High Celebrations of the Holy Eucharist, Coronations and the ceremonies of the Ordination of Priests and the Consecration of Bishops.

World figures who displayed the qualities of the sixth Ray are referred to in the Chapter on blended Rays.

CHAPTER VIII

THE SEVENTH RAY

THE special qualities of the seventh Ray are nobility and chivalry both of character and conduct, splendour of estate and person, ordered activity, precision, skill, grace, dignity, great interest in politics, the arts, ceremonial pageantry, magic, the discovery, control and release of the hidden forces of Nature and co-operation with the Intelligences associated with them.

The type of man is the politician—in the true meaning of the word—stage director, pageant master, ritualist, magician, occultist and Priest in ceremonial Orders.

The ideals are power perfectly and irresistibly made manifest, true aristocracy both of body and mind, physical efficiency, perfection, matter-of-factness and order in all the conduct of life, perfect tidiness of appointments, unquestioned power to control and direct the hidden forces of the person's own nature and of Nature herself, the whole being inspired and rendered irresistible by the force of a will which is relatively omnipotent. A seventh Ray motto would be: " If a thing is worth doing, it is worth doing well." This would apply equally to a picnic or a pageant, a poem

or a parade, a military tournament or a magical rite.
God, for the seventh Ray man, is the principle of Order
in all things, and chaos is the greatest evil. The driving
impulse is to harness and make manifest with precision
according to a design the forces and intelligences of
Nature.

Results are obtained by synthesising a number of
factors to produce a clearly conceived result. The
formation of groups of people to be trained and led in
co-ordinated activity in politics, in various branches of
the arts, in pageantry, the drama and opera, is an
example of this method, as also in the use of vestments,
colours, symbols, and of signs and words of power in
ceremonial. As teacher, he makes full use of the
drama, both in personal presentations and in school
technique. He also employs the methods of the first
Ray. The apotheosis is dual, namely, to become a
spiritual magician, and to live perfectly down to the
smallest detail. Freemasonry is both a ceremonial and
a practical expression of one attribute of the seventh
Ray, which is also represented in the rituals of all
World Faiths.

Amongst the defects of the type are ostentation, pre-
tentiousness, unscrupulousness, love of power and office,
readiness to use people as tools, " dead letter "
formalism and the mechanical performance of cere-
mony to the neglect of its spiritual significance, and
a tendency to descend into black magic, sorcery, necro-
mancy and the baser forms of priestcraft. Seventh
Ray people can suffer acutely under humiliation,

loss of outer power, adverse criticism, particularly from one of a lesser degree, and subjection to rude behaviour.

The principle of man is the physical body. The colours are purple and sapphire blue, the jewel is the amethyst and the symbols are the clockwise-turning swastika and the seven-pointed star. The correspondence is with the first Ray, the seventh representing the power of that Ray expressed in physical action. Of the Arts, sculpture—frozen dancing—represents the seventh Ray.

The general influence of the seventh Ray upon humanity is said now to be displacing that of the sixth, with consequent tendencies in science to explore the normally invisible universe, as by the radio telescope, to investigate the extra sensory powers and *psyche* of man as in ESP [1] and psychosomatic medicine, and to tap and use the hidden forces of Nature as in nuclear fission. In public life this influence is observable in the prevalent liking for pageantry and ceremonial. In the Christian religion the effect of the seventh Ray is discernible in the movement towards High Church as in Anglo-Catholicism, in a deepening recognition of the spiritual significance and efficacy of ceremonial, in movements towards co-operation between sects and in attempts to establish a brotherhood of World Faiths or Parliament of Religions (2nd Ray—co-operation, 7th Ray—co-ordination). In world affairs, as the

[1] Vide *The Reach of the Mind*, J. B. Rhine.

qualities of the second and third Rays are also developing, the growing influence of the seventh Ray increases
the tendency to substitute arbitration and co-operation
for force as a means of settling disputes.   As the influence of the Ray grows stronger and is supplemented
by an appropriate development of the higher, synthesising mind of man, these tendencies will become
stronger, eventually making fully effective the ideals
upon which UNO and such subsidiaries as UNESCO
and UNRRA, and Marshall Aid, local Defence Pacts
and World Conferences are founded.

CHAPTER IX

BLENDED RAYS

READERS who, by the application of this information to their own personalities as they know them, have been endeavouring to discover their own Rays, will possibly find themselves to be displaying the qualities of more than one, no special Ray characteristics appearing to predominate. If, however, they will examine themselves closely they will generally find that in the means by which they obtain desired results, they tend to employ fairly consistently the method of one or another of the Rays.

As has been suggested, affinities or correspondences exist between the Rays. The first and the seventh Rays are intimately associated, as also are the second and the sixth and the third and the fifth. In addition, the first three Rays, which are life Rays, may be regarded as the spiritual ensoulment of the last three, which are Rays of form. The fourth Ray corresponds to the natural bridge or pathway, both between each related pair and the two sets of three.

Since the goal is the full development of all the qualities of all the Rays, it is, however, necessary that the activities and developments of the long series of lives [1] on earth should include all of their characteristics. This is exemplified in the lives of the greater figures of history, most of whom displayed the blended qualities of two and sometimes more Rays. The Pharaohs, Alexanders, Caesars and Napoleons of the world, for example, manifested predominantly the power aspect of the first Ray. A study of their lives reveals, however, marked differences between them, according to the degree in which the qualities of other Rays were blended with those of the first Ray.

Richard Wagner would seem to have displayed predominantly the qualities of the fourth and the seventh Rays; he was an artist who combined many branches of the Arts in ceremonial portrayals of occult and spiritual truths. He was also a poet, dramatist, philosopher and splendid prose writer (3rd Ray). To produce a chosen effect in his operas he blended into a unity these diverse faculties (7th Ray). The mystical impulse was embedded in his fiery soul (6th Ray). His music and message reveal the truth that each individual soul is at one with the World Soul, and must ultimately realise that unity (2nd Ray). He was amongst the first to portray, as in the Love Duet in *Tristram and Isolde*, the exaltation of human love into a spiritual experience of unity (2nd Ray). In order to attain these objectives, Wagner had to explore and present new art forms, to break existing barriers and

---

[1] The doctrine of man's spiritual evolution by means of successive lives on earth, or Reincarnation, is implicit throughout this work. Vide *Reincarnation, Fact or Fallacy?*, Geoffrey Hodson.

set music free (1st Ray). He was deeply moved by the idea of the formation of a great Brotherhood of Arts (2nd Ray), and his whole life was devoted to the regeneration of the human race, using the Arts as means of accomplishment (6th and 4th Rays).

Wagner was also a great humanitarian, his love overflowing to the members of the Animal Kingdom. His letters contain charming references to animal pets and one of his Essays is directed against vivisection (2nd and 6th Rays). He enriched humanity with the sublime conception of human life as an ascent of the Soul to perfection (3rd Ray), shed upon it the beauty of his melodies and harmonies (4th Ray) and displayed a remarkable power to move the human heart (2nd, 6th and 7th Rays). Within his work are to be found treasures of wisdom and beauty (2nd and 4th Rays). An occult tradition states that he was a reincarnation of Sophocles, the great Greek dramatist.

Leonardo da Vinci (1452-1519) is best known for his paintings, especially the Louvre's " Mona Lisa "; he was also very successful as scientist, inventor and prophet. In these he displayed the qualities of the 4th, 5th and 3rd Rays respectively. He would seem to have been aware of the heliocentric system some thirty years before Copernicus publicly affirmed it (5th Ray). He was learned in philosophy (3rd Ray), anatomy, astronomy, botany, natural science, medicine, optical science, meteorology, and even aviation—all 5th Ray activities. He achieved great results in these fields and passed on knowledge which is still being used by modern scientists   He was well versed in architecture (6th Ray), music (4th Ray) and warfare (1st Ray). He made plans for the mass production of guns, ammunition and another weapon which might be regarded as the ancestor of the tank.

Da Vinci made a careful study of the life and the wing and feather movements of birds, seeking to wrest from them the secret of their flight. Modern aircraft construction does not diverge unduly from the lines he laid down. One of his water turbines is almost modern in construction, as are his odometer—a device to measure distances by counting the turns of a wheel—and his mechanical jack. He designed a paddle wheel boat, a cantilever swing bridge, a self-propelled car, devised roller bearings and built waterways, using canal lock systems still in use today at Milan and in the Panama Canal. He was therefore an outstanding example of the blending of the 3rd, 4th and 5th Rays in one highly developed individual, and was in no wise deficient in the powers and qualities of the other four Rays.

The work and thought of the abstractionist, Josef Albers (born in Westphalia 1889) illustrates the effect of a blending of the 3rd, 4th and 5th Rays in an artist. His works are described (*Time*, January 31st, 1949) as " emotionless abstractions, composed mostly of straight lines and right angles thinly painted in pure colours. At first glance his paintings look rigid and definite to the point of dullness, but there is nothing definite about them.   Through tricks of contrast and perspective, he makes the shapes in his painting shift and change as one looks at them, even makes the colours take on varying hues. ' Oh, you see, I want my inventions to act, to lose their identity. What I expect from my colours and forms is that they do something they do not want to do themselves. For instance, I want to push a green so it looks red. . . . All my work is experimental. . . . When people say my paintings have no emotion, I agree. I say . . . precision can make you crazy too. A locomotive is without emotion as is a mathematics book but they are exciting to me ' " (5th Ray).

Clement Richard Attlee, Britain's Prime Minister from 1945, is described (by the London *Observer's* Diplomatic Correspondent in *The New Zealand Herald*, 20-1-49) as " a competent and conciliatory chairman, holding office not by reason of positive qualities of his own, but as an intermediary (3rd Ray). . . . Yet he is today the complete master of his Cabinet and he has quietly carried through changes in Cabinet structure which place in his hand more of the strings of power than have ever before been held by a British Prime Minister in peacetime (1st and 3rd Rays). . . .

" The secret of Attlee's power is often sought in his great integrity. But . . . the secret lies deeper. Attlee's strength comes from a peculiar form of disciplined independence (1st, 3rd, 5th and 7th Rays). . . . Attlee is completely self-sustained. He is not afflicted by unpopularity. He is, in fundamental decisions, even unaffected by the approval or disapproval of intimates of whom indeed he has few (1st and 3rd Rays). . . . He has something of that quality of private decision, that ability to follow his own analysis of events to its logical conclusion, unperturbed by the feelings of those around him, unperturbed, also, by his own feelings, fears or vanities. (1st, 3rd and 5th Rays). . . . A politician, to manœuvre, also needs tactical skill and a quiet nimbleness (3rd, 5th and 7th Rays). Here, again, Attlee is surprisingly well equipped. He has successfully ridden even revolt in his party, chiefly, by remarkable timing —by knowing when to remain quiescent and when to bring the issue to a climax (3rd and 5th Rays).

"Those who have challenged him are never quite sure just how they were defeated (3rd Ray). Moreover, he has . . . an almost instinctive awareness of the reactions of the rank and file of his party and of the country at large (2nd and 3rd Rays).

"He quietly became a Socialist, opposing his family (his father was a Gladstonian Liberal) by carrying his own ideas to their logical conclusions (3rd and 5th Rays).

"Clement actually went to live among the East Enders (poorer peoples of London) and in the embryonic Labour movement he 'found himself.' He had, so to speak, emigrated to a new world of his own choice (1st Ray). He brought intact his habits of loyalty (6th Ray), his idealism and his capacity for leadership (1st Ray) and formed a union with the East End which is still the warmest and happiest element in his life (2nd and 6th Rays). . . .

" The Labour Party was in an almost hopeless mess
—utterly defeated and divided into quarrelling factions.
Attlee, loyal (6th Ray), modest, impartial (3rd Ray),
clear-headed (5th Ray), capable of decision (1st Ray)
and with the courage of his personal detachment (1st
and 3rd Rays), had precisely the qualities needed. . . .
He has proved himself capable of much, including a
feat of imaginative statesmanship—his astounding solution of the Indian dilemma (1st, 3rd and 5th Rays)."

General Booth, founder of the Salvation Army, a
man of great power, quenchless enthusiasm and immense fervour, was an example of the blend of the
qualities of the first and sixth Rays. Quite naturally,
his fiery faith and burning ardour to save souls
(6th and 2nd Rays) found expression in active warfare
against evil (1st Ray). He named his Magazine *The
War Cry* and took his followers—organised into and
named an " Army "—into action with flags, uniforms,
bands, drums, cymbals and all the panoply of war.
In many cities the headquarters of the Salvation Army
is named " The Citadel ".   Of interest, in view of the
colours appropriate to the Rays, is the fact that for the
most part the colour of the Salvation Army, as on uniforms and banners, is red.

Cardinal Manning—a great admirer of General
Booth—was also an example of blended sixth and first
Rays. He was by instinct not a theologian as was
Cardinal Newman—scholar and recluse (blended 5th
and 3rd Rays)—but a crusader (6th Ray). Like
General Booth, Cardinal Manning also saw religion as

a warfare for the salvation of souls. He craved power
to wage the war effectively and was obsessed with the
responsibility of rule. He might be called a spiritual
imperialist. He was a born General and embarked
upon an aggressive campaign of Catholic expansion
(1st Ray). Newman, with his passion for truth and
free enquiry (3rd and 5th Ray), saw the Church as a
University. Manning, with his passion for victory,
saw it as an army with ranks closed against questioning,
because it weakened resolution (1st Ray). Time,
whilst acknowledging Manning's greatness, has proved
Newman right and Manning wrong. The prosperous
Catholic foundations in Oxford testify to the rightness
of Newman's belief in knowledge (5th Ray), understanding (3rd Ray), and religious experience (2nd, 4th
and 6th Rays) as the greatest powers with which to
wage war against evil. The lives and characters of
these three men suggest that in General Booth the sixth
Ray was predominant, with the first splendidly
developed, whilst in Cardinals Manning and Newman
the first and the third Rays respectively predominated
over the sixth.

Hypatia (martyred 415 A. D.) [1] and Giordano Bruno
(1548-1600), [2] reincarnations, we are informed, of the
same Ego, both displayed marked sixth Ray attributes,
matched and tempered by an unusual development of

[1] A woman teacher of Greek philosophy in Alexandria, distin-
guished for her wisdom, beauty and purity of life.

[2] Described as a fervid original thinker who regarded God as
the living omnipresent Soul of the universe and Nature as the living
garment of God.

the qualities and powers of the third and fifth Rays. In addition, each of these great souls possessed the fourth Ray power of magnificent oratory and literary craftsmanship. Their lives were terminated in martyr-dom, displaying the typical sixth Ray quality of readiness to endure all, sacrifice all, including life itself, for an ideal and a cause.

Pythagoras (540-510 B.C.), Greek philosopher and founder of the Pythagorean school, who is credited with the discovery of the theorem that the square of the hypotenuse of a right-angled triangle is equal to the sum of the squares of the other two sides, the helio-centric system and the mathematical principles of music, displayed to a remarkable degree the intellectual powers, of the third and fifth Rays, combining with them great capacities as a teacher. An occult tradi-tion states that he has attained Adeptship and now also shows forth to a very high degree the second Ray qualities of wisdom, love and compassion.

Queen Victoria is said to be a reincarnation of King Alfred; both were great monarchs and splendid first Ray types. Tennyson is similarly associated with Virgil, each being a poet (3rd Ray) and an artist (4th Ray) and attaining to lofty mystical experience (2nd and 6th Rays). Gladstone, egoically identified with Cicero, the Roman orator, statesman and man of letters (106-42 B.C.), in both incarnations manifested the qualities of the first, third, fourth and seventh Rays.

Every successful artist, for whom love of beauty and the aspiration to portray it perfectly come first in life, is either a fourth Ray individual or has developed to a high degree the qualities of that Ray. The choice of a branch or branches of the Arts, of media and modes of creative self-expression and performance, is likely to be decided by the influence of the sub-dominant Ray. Of these, the first and seventh Rays would tend towards dancing and sculpture. Each of these in turn would show the effect of the Ray influence. Ballet, for example, has been described as a seventh Ray art, whilst solo dancing indicates the first Ray.

Second and sixth Ray developments in artists' character would lead them towards music and architecture, each branch in its turn being affected by the developed tendencies of other Rays. The great composers differ markedly in the quality of their compositions, but in all of them the third and fifth Rays also must be well developed to provide the capacity to conceive abstract ideas and to express them in obedience to mathematical laws.

Artists with the third and fifth Rays as sub-dominant influences take naturally to literature and painting, those choices in their turn being expressed according to the influence of other Rays. The markedly fourth Ray writer might excel in poetry, whilst the pure thinker, the philosopher and the scientist might prefer the freedom of prose.

The first Ray painter will deal more with bold masses than with intricate detail, whilst the fifth Ray painter would be more likely to employ the latter. Abstractionism in an artist indicates strong third Ray

5

tendencies, whilst unmistakable clarity and intention would indicate the influence of the fifth Ray. The pure artist will possess the power of enchantment. By sheer beauty he will charm and delight those responsive to his influence.

Perfect examples of complete development along the lines of one Ray are provided in the lives and persons of the Lord Christ and the Lord Buddha. Throughout the whole of Their ministries They displayed in the highest degree the wisdom, the compassion, the love and the abiding sense of unity with all people characteristic of the second Ray. The correspondence with the sixth Ray emerged in the manner of the death of Christ, in which He sacrificed life itself for the truths He came to teach, notably those of brotherly love and self-sacrifice.

If, with the utmost reverence, one may presume to say so, with Their great Predecessor, the Lord Shri Krishna, these exalted Personages also expressed in Their highest forms the qualities and powers of the other five Rays: for They were master leaders of men (1st Ray); master philosophers possessed of complete comprehension (3rd Ray); master artists in the beauty of Their lives, Their teaching and the language in which it was invariably clothed (4th Ray); master scientists possessing both profound knowledge, physical and superphysical, and the power to demonstrate it (5th Ray); perfect embodiments of lofty idealism with the power to evoke it in others (6th Ray); master magicians, especially in the greatest of all magic, the transformation of the character and lives of human beings (7th Ray). All men will one day attain to comparable sevenfold development, though the qualities of the Monadic Ray will still predominate.

CHAPTER X

THE PERSONAL RAY

THE seven principles or components of the human individuality may be regarded as vehicles through which self-expression and experience are gained by that unit of spiritual existence which is sometimes called the Monad. Other titles are Spark of the One Divine Flame, Breath of the Great Breath, Scintilla of the Spiritual Sun, Immortal Germ, Human Spirit, Logos of the Soul. All of these describe, however imperfectly, aspects of the mysterious Dweller in the Innermost which is at once a unit and an inseparable part of Universal Spirit.

The Monad is regarded as the source of the objective, sevenfold human being. As the name Immortal Germ indicates, it is also a seed of the Divine "Tree of Life", containing within itself the potentiality of all the powers of that parent Tree which is the transcendent and immanent Godhead.

The Monad, it is said, never leaves "the bosom of the Father". The Divine Spirit of man remains within the parent Flame throughout the whole period of its partial manifestations as a sevenfold human being. It does, however, radiate or project a ray of its own Power, Life and Light into the objective universe which is its evolutionary field. This Monadic Ray shines forth through one of the three aspects of the triune Deity and thereafter through one or other of the seven Archangelic Beings through which that Deity becomes externally manifest as the Emanator and Architect of a universe.

In consequence of these intimate associations, the objective expression of the human Monad becomes coloured or imprinted with the attributes of that Aspect of Deity and of that Archangel through which it shines forth. Thus, while the whole potentiality is present in every Monad in all subsequent self-manifestations, one attribute will be accentuated, one quality preponderate.

In order to discover with certainty either one's own Ray or that of another person, it would therefore be necessary to ascend in consciousness to the Monad itself, or at least to the highest expression of its present individuality, that, of Spiritual Will or *Atma*; for there the Ray colouring, the Sephirothal imprint, would be apparent. Only a highly developed occultist and seer is capable of making this investigation.

Since, however, Ray qualities begin to show themselves fairly clearly in human beings of the present evolutionary age, careful examination of character will generally provide fairly trustworthy indications of a person's Ray. When attempting this, it is important to remember that whilst the attributes and qualities of each of the seven Rays are present in every individual, in order to achieve all-round development the predominating Ray and Ray activity of the outer personality may change life after life or even during one life. In consequence, it is often very difficult to decide upon one's own or another person's Monadic Ray. There are, however, certain indications which may possibly lead to the discovery of one's Ray. Amongst these are the predominant quality in one's character, that most admired in the character of others, the driving impulse or chief purpose in life, the method of obtaining desired results and the outstanding weaknesses, particularly those found to be the most difficult to eradicate.

Until Adeptship is closely approached, nearly everyone will be likely to display inequalities of development. Whilst virtuosity may be shown in some directions, exceptional ability and noble qualities in others, marked limitations may also be discernible. Pettiness in some personal matters can show itself in otherwise great people. Miscalculation and unwisdom can mould the judgment and reduce the effectiveness of those who can at times display statesmanship of the highest order. Thus in the character of very great, but still imperfect, men and women there are mountains and valleys, as it were. Those who are passing through earlier evolutionary phases will tend generally to display the defects rather than the desirable qualities of the Rays, their vices rather than their virtues, even though the latter may shine out on certain occasions.

Egoic development or, as it is sometimes called, age of the Soul, is decisive in ability to overcome weaknesses. Only well-developed or " old Souls " will either be interested in doing so or possess the power to succeed. The time required to overcome a defect, once it is recognized, is similarly dependent upon evolutionary age, the more advanced often proving able instantly to check the expression of an undesirable characteristic and quickly to achieve its elimination.

In other words, the number of earthly lives and the progress made in most of them decide whether the strengths or the weaknesses, the virtues or the vices, the positive or negative aspects of the Ray attributes will find predominant expression in habitual thought, motive, feelings and actions.

If the following attributes of Fifth Ray people are notable features of a person's character, then it would be fair to assume a first Ray individuality: will power, determination, and a tendency to override the wishes and limit the freedom of others; ardent wish for positions of power and a natural capacity to rule and lead; the use of superior force in most emergencies, often without regard for the feelings of others, and a tendency to sulk when obstructed.

Recognition of the fact that happiness depends upon freedom of thought and action; readiness to grant that freedom; a capacity to make wise decisions and plans; a universality of affection; a great desire to save, uplift and bestow happiness upon others, particularly by sharing possessions; a gift of teaching and a preference for winning enemies over so that they become friends and collaborators, and the weaknesses of sentimentality and sensuality—if these are displayed in any one person, then they may fairly be regarded as being on the second Ray.

If the ready comprehension of abstract ideas and of the meaning, intention and character of people; the faculty of impartial examination; adaptability and tact; capacity to organise, plan and order with far-seeing intelligence and play a good game of chess; the love of philosophy; admiration for great philosophers and strategists; a readiness to comprehend and explain varied phenomena by reference to a fundamental principle; ability to engage in prolonged contempla-tion, and, on occasion, indecision, aloofness and a tendency to intrigue even to the extent of unscrupulous deceit, are marked characteristics of one's nature, then one is probably on the third Ray.

If love of beauty and harmony, and a natural sense of rhythm and balance; a life devoted to one or other of the Arts; an aspiration to shed beauty upon the world; a tendency to dramatise and illustrate expound-ed ideas with rhythmic forms; a certain power of allurement, and the weaknesses of self-conceit, self-indulgence and surrender to moods, are outstanding qualities, then the fourth Ray is indicated.

If the mind is analytical and legal, prizing logic above all else; the scientific method of thought strongly appeals and the establishment of incontrovertible facts is a driving impulse; charts and diagrams are used in study and teaching; and the analytical mind is used in perpetual probing and searching for ultimate fact, and the weaknesses of egoism, excessive criticism of others, self-righteousness, pedantry, narrowness, materialism, and prying inquisitiveness, are marked characteristics, then fifth Ray qualities are being displayed.

If fiery enthusiasm; a strong sense of loyalty; a certain single-mindedness in everything that is thought and done; and capacity for devotion and self-sacrifice, particularly in service; if resolve burns within one as an irresistible spiritual power, and the weaknesses of emotionalism, impulsiveness, fanaticism and sensuality are consistently displayed, then the sixth Ray predominates.

If one is attracted to occult science and its expression through ceremonial and magic and has a highly developed sense of order, system and method; if one likes to combine a number of influences in order to give expression to ideas and successfully appeal to the senses and intellect; if grace and splendour and the ideals of chivalry and knightliness make strong appeal; if the instinct to harness invisible forces for the fulfilment of human needs, and the weaknesses of formalism and of love of power and office are all marks of one's nature, then one is evolving, at least for the time being, on the seventh Ray.

The true Ray, it should be remembered, may only be known after correct assessment of the quality, nature and influence of the Monad itself, the Dweller in the Innermost which first received the imprint and colour of one or other of the Seven Mighty Spirits before the Throne.

The Ray of the Ego is that of the Monad also, but in the course of its evolution the Ego expresses through its successive personalities—and therefore appears to display predominantly—the qualities and powers of Ray after Ray. A study of the Ego through a number of such incarnations would doubtless reveal one central quality or light shining through all major activities and achievements, and this would indicate the Monadic Ray.

Each Personality in its turn is influenced by both single Rays and combinations, producing in human nature a great variety of characteristics, capacities and weaknesses. Even so, a completely dispassionate observance of persisting basic tendencies, particularly in the choice of that which is most admired and the method of obtaining desired results, will generally reveal the Monadic Ray.

Let us, for example, follow seven different types of people into a store and note their shopping methods. If a customer strides in with pre-determined choice, goes direct to the department and counter where it is to be obtained, gives the order in a few words, waits calmly whilst it is wrapped up, pays, and strides out again, not looking particularly to the right or left, then first Ray characteristics have been displayed. If, furthermore, a certain amount of force has been used to reach the counter or even the foremost possible place in a queue, and if the needs of both fellow-shoppers and assistants are but little considered and a certain curtness is evidenced, these indications would confirm the decision.

If, on the other hand, due consideration is given to the wishes and priority of other purchasers and the fatigued or harassed condition of the person who is serving is observed, sympathized with and allowed for; if an attempt is made to win his or her co-operation and help, as by means of a description of the purposes for which the articles are being purchased, and if failure to obtain what was required after giving considerable trouble is followed either by an apology or the purchase of unwanted goods in recompense, then that person would probably be on the second Ray.

The third Ray individual would probably have especial regard for the place of the merchandise in a general scheme, as of interior decoration or dress. He would also have formed a clear idea of the material, texture, style and colour of his purchase. Choosing and entering the particular store in which the article is most likely to be available, his procedure would be strictly impersonal, all proffered goods being accepted or rejected entirely upon grounds of suitability. Should the right article be found, the third Ray purchaser would generally be ready to pay the required price. Unless the fifth Ray is also strong in him, he is not inclined to haggle over prices or be influenced in his choice by the thought of obtaining a bargain. If the shop assistants are unable to produce the desired goods, then, without much regard for their feelings, the shopper would decline to purchase.

The fourth Ray person is most likely to be concerned with the beauty of the objects to be purchased. Whilst capable of employing the method of any of the Rays in planning, carrying out and completing a shopping expedition, the decisive factor would be loveliness, charm. The treatment of the assistant would depend almost entirely upon the mood or the physical condition of the purchaser at the moment, and could vary from winning friendliness to complete disregard of any other feelings than his own. In the personal choice of colour, background assumes considerable significance. Certain hues and shades are skilfully blended to produce an effective colour scheme. The sub-Rays would be likely to influence the choice of these colours, though the true artist would probably be willing to use any colour in any shade in order to achieve a desired effect.

Close attention to detail is likely to be exhibited by fifth Ray people. Not only will the general plan of operation have been clearly formed, but the precise colour, shape and size of the article or material will have been decided upon. A pattern or sample of both texture and colour will often be used as a guide, with considerable insistence upon exactitude in such matters. Price is important, and sometimes the cheapness of goods or the possibility of a bargain will influence the choice. Comparisons with similar goods in other shops are likely to be made, and the cheapest of them

patronised. As nearly as possible, the exact amount
of money will be tendered, and where change is required
it will be carefully checked.

Shopping expeditions can make considerable demands upon the patience of those whose aid is sought
by fifth Ray people in finding and buying goods. Even
though the desired article is found in the first shop
which is visited, a tour must still be made of the other
stores where goods which are almost as suitable may
prove to be on sale. The resultant confusion and
indecision can be very exasperating, particularly to
friends in whom the first and seventh Rays combine to
bestow the capacity for making quick decisions.

Warmth of colour would probably be sought by
those on the sixth Ray, as also by their brothers on the
second. Unless pursuing one-pointedly a single idea
or temporarily driven by an overmastering desire, they
will be kindly and considerate in their relations with
the shop assistant. They are universal rather than
particular in their choice of both goods and store, and
are likely to be influenced by what they see on display
or what is pressed upon them by persuasive salesmen.
They would probably not be nearly as decisive in such
matters as those influenced by the first, third and fifth
Rays and could, in consequence, be somewhat difficult
people to serve. They tend to be affected by occur-
rences during the shopping expedition and especially
by the treatment they receive from both fellow-shoppers
and assistants. Annoying circumstances might cause
them to act quite illogically, even to the extent of

refusing out of pique to purchase an obviously suitable article.

Seventh Ray people would tend to seek perfection in whatever is purchased, particularly in personal attire, adornment and in the decoration of a home. They might, indeed, justly be described as perfectionists. Beauty, grace, fitness and a certain splendour are their notable characteristics. They resemble their brothers of the first Ray in their relationship with their fellows and are naturally courteous, considerate and appreciative of those with whom they deal. Price influences them hardly at all, and they are inclined to tender a larger sum than is required and to accept their change without putting themselves to too much trouble in counting it. There is a certain princely largesse in the character and conduct of people on the seventh Ray.

One particular quality is generally regarded as supremely desirable by persons on each of the seven Rays. For the first Ray this is power; for the second, wisdom; for the third, comprehension; for the fourth, beauty; for the fifth, knowledge; for the sixth, one-pointed devotion; and for the seventh, order.

Knowledge of the seven Rays is helpful in the comprehension of others, especially of those whose approach to life, methods of obtaining desired ends and ultimate destiny differ from one's own. Such knowledge can bestow upon those who possess it one of the highest virtues. This is a wide tolerance, born of deep understanding, concerning the ideals and actions of other nations and of other individuals. This virtue is beautifully expressed in the words of the Lord Shri Krishna, who was speaking as an incarnation of Vishnu, the Second Aspect of the Blessed Trinity:

" However men approach Me, even so do I welcome them, for the path men take from every side is Mine." (*Bhagavad Gita*, IV, 11, translated by Annie Besant.)